Kingdom Leadership

Written by: Carlton Christ Evans, Jr.

Kingdom Leadership

Copyright Page

Kingdom Leadership
Written by: Carlton Christ Evans, Jr.

Copyright © 2021 by: Carlton Christ Evans, Jr.
All Rights Reserved.

Published by: Rise Publishing Company

ISBN: 978-1-959080-00-8
Printed in the United States of America.

All rights reserved. No part of this publication may be reproduced, stored in a retrieval system, or transmitted in any form or by any means – electronic, mechanical, photocopy, recording, scanning, or otherwise – without the prior written consent of the publisher, except by provided by the United States of America copyright law.

Unless otherwise noted, scripture quotations are taken from the New King James Version®. ©1982 by Thomas Nelson. Used by permission. All rights reserved.

The Holy Bible, 21st Century King James Version® (KJ21®) Copyright ©1994 by Deuel Enterprises, Inc., Gary, SD 57237. All rights reserved.

Scripture taken from *The Message*. Copyright © 1993, 1994, 1995, 1996, 2000, 2001, 2002. Used by permission of NavPress Publishing Group.

Previously published as Spiritual Leadership Manual by Carlton Christ Evans, Jr.

Rise Publishing Company
www.RisePublishingCompany.com

Table of Contents

Introduction 7

1) Spiritual Foundation 9

2) Lifestyle of Prayer 29

3) The Bible 39

4) Discipleship 53

5) The Church 71

6) The Kingdom of God 85

Introduction

God prompted me to write this manual because of the current state of what is known as *church* and *ministry*. Also, God is producing vast impact and changes within the Body of Christ, and He is doing so globally. Therefore, God instructed me to write this manual.

In mid-November of 2020, God showed me in a dream that most of the spiritual leadership positions within His Kingdom are changing. Then God spoke to me and said, "Son, it is not that there is a void of qualified spiritual leaders. There are simply too many unqualified and disqualified spiritual leaders in churches and ministries." This manual will provide a clear understanding and paint a vivid picture of what is currently happening with spiritual leadership, what it will look like, and what you need to look for in spiritual leadership.

1

Spiritual Foundation

The biggest unlearned and unanswered question is the order of God. Many have pondered, what came first, a man or a church? A woman or a church? Children or church? Etc. Many simply do not know nor understand God's divine will nor His order as it deals with the family nucleus and the church.

In Genesis, there was a man and a woman who came together in a union of marriage. They procreated as God blessed and commanded them (see Gen. 1:26-28). The first institution in the world and the beginning of humanity was man, woman, children, and family. From the genesis, the family has always preceded the church. So what do you think are God's priorities? God's priority will always be people and, more specifically, the family unit. However, people are more focused on structures, institutions, organizations, denominations, and tribes. Such is not so with God. God is most concerned about the family unit because it impacts the soul of a person.

The Nucleus

Unbeknownst to many, spiritual leadership starts in the home. The cause for so much dysfunction and confusion in our world is rooted within the homes. The Bible says, "For if a man does not know how to rule his own house, how will he take care of the church of God?" (1 Tim. 3:5). Therefore, if a man leads his home poorly or does not provide for his family, he is worse than an infidel (1 Tim. 5:8, paraphrased).

As of late, people's focus has been on the wrong things. Instead of being attentive to their homes, many have shown more passion toward the things of the demonic, wickedness, status quo, and rank. People are not focused on becoming the image and likeness of Christ, nor are they willing to be the example of being Christ-like.

Being like Christ begins in the home because spiritual leadership must start at home. If you wonder why there is so much dysfunction in some houses of worship, look no further than this subject. A lot of dysfunction is in the church because there is a lot of dysfunction in the family unit. Many family units have resorted to turning a blind eye to overcome negativity and unresolved problems.

As a result, this is reflected in the church. It is no wonder there are so many broken people in the church. It is no wonder there is a constant influx of single and remarried people. The disunity that has originated in the home manifested itself in the ecclesia.

However, God wants to deal with the disunity, dysfunction, and disconnect within His people. But He requires our participation. We, as God's children, must be honest and deal with the issues that need to be resolved. We can no longer sweep our issues under the rug and pretend they do not exist. God is concerned about solving the problems that are plaguing our world. The church is a vital element, so He is starting within His people. God has called us to a higher degree, and we must be whole and healed. We, the people of God, are vital. For the church is in the front line of this world.

Where Is Your Focus?

The focus and priorities of people are entirely different from the priorities of God. God is most concerned about the spiritual fax, the spiritual health of His leaders. Yet many are unaware of this truth. Fortunately, God is raising spiritual leaders who know His Word and have His heart, as is in Jeremiah 3:15. These individuals are leaders who understand what leadership entails. Leadership is about knowing and possessing the priorities of God while keeping the focus on God.

If a leader does not have the priorities of God, then what can that leader do for you? What can they be to you within the capacity of leadership? Nothing. Sadly, we see an influx of unqualified people being reproduced simply because of their connection. You cannot be connected to ill-equipped leaders and expect to walk as a quality person in the eyes of God. Only quality can reproduce quality.

If your leader's life is always in disarray, no matter how eloquently they speak or how good they look in the public eye, the spirit that is in them will manifest within you. The same spirit of dysfunction will be imparted to those who are connected. Thus, you must be discerning and flee from such leaders and persons.

The Reestablishment of God's Priorities

With this manual, God is using me to reintroduce and reestablish His priorities within the church and the Body of Christ. With that said, we must note that God's priority is establishing a relationship with His sons and daughters. Unfortunately, most people are not experiencing the fullness of having a relationship with God, as He intended. Many believe that saying, "I believe in God," establishes a solid relationship with God. However, it is not sufficient in God's eye to merely express your belief in Him. Your verbal declaration concerning your faith will not make an impact nor an effectual change.

Many people profess the name of Jesus Christ, yet their actions do not align with His Word. In the Words of the Bible, these kinds of people have a form of godliness but deny its power. With these types of people, we must turn away and have no parts nor relations (2 Tim.

3:5). The fullness of 2 Timothy 3:5 is an expression of carnality—living a life of worldliness. Sadly, those who only profess their love for Christ are like those who will never show admonition to the Father. Those we speak of fall into the same category as atheists and agnostics, and religious people.

<u>Varying Beliefs</u>

Atheism is the belief that God does not exist. Agnostics believe that there is a supreme being, something beyond the natural, but not God. Then there are the religious people. Those who are religious believe there is a God but do not have a revelation nor a genuine relationship with God.

The cause for these various belief systems is the lack of revelation on the Kingdom of God. You need revelation. If you do not have a revelation of the Kingdom of God, then you do not know God. It is impossible to know God if you do not have an authentic relationship with Him and if you do not have knowledge of His Kingdom. To know God's Kingdom is to be full of His Word. Psalm 138:2 says God has magnified His Word above His name. Therefore, the root of truly knowing God and building a relationship with Him rests in His Word. Above all else, God prioritizes the His Word; without it, you will be void of Him.

Do You Really Know Him?

About four to six years ago, the Lord told me that about 88 percent of the people in the nation do not know Him. In that percentage, think about how many people go to church, how many people are religious, and say they believe and know God. Yet God said 88 percent of them do not know Him.

We are talking about those who acknowledge some type of supernatural or supreme being, something beyond what we see naturally. Then you have religious people who say they believe in God but traditionally serve God, a way not prescribed according to Scripture. It should make you wonder. If God said 88 percent of the nation does not know Him, then who is everyone serving? The method of most people's servitude is derived from a place of carnality. It is birth from the flesh, derived from the soul, and is not spiritual. Only if you are born-again can you truly worship God in spirit and truth. I urge you, do not be an 88 percenter that does not know God. Become born-again, genuinely love the Lord, and carry the heart of the Father.

Leaders after God's Own Heart

Leaders must have God's vision, knowledge, and comprehension and the ability to lead His people into their victory and promise. God wants His children to walk into their destiny and the glory that He has for them. However, it is essential to note that God wants His children to go forth in their callings and as the Body of

Christ. Therefore, God is raising people who are capable, ready, and trained and possess His heart.

We must understand that God's leaders will never be elected, voted in, or selected by people's opinions, race, religious affiliations, nor organizations. It has nothing to do with worldly ways. Instead, God chooses who He has anointed, appointed, equipped, prepared, tested, and proven for their work in ministry.

I remember earlier in my walk with Christ, and before I had my children, I asked God to help me be a father to my children and the father they deserved. I did not approach fatherhood through my perception of being a father nor the world's standards of what fatherhood entails. I asked God to make me the father my children needed and for me to represent God the best way I could.

I know I have been an excellent father to my children because they are very prosperous and fruitful. They are not perfect, but they are doing well in their lives. My children are well-rounded, intelligent, and very proficient in their vocations. Not to mention, they are wise, insightful, and responsible. That is the kind of children God created because, as their first leader, I am a conduit connecting them to the Holy Spirit who empowers them as they are connected to me.

Because I am connected to the Source—God—I led my children into blessings, prosperity, and victory. Additionally, I had the privilege of introducing them to Jesus, which allowed them to desire God, love

God, and know that God is real. My exemplary leadership has availed them to see life, God, and themselves properly.

Heart Is the Passion

In regard to having heart and passion, we can look to hard-working technology giant moguls and athletes as examples. Many people are aware of successful moguls like Mark Zuckerberg with Facebook, Steve Jobs with Apple, and Bill Gates with Microsoft, as well as famous athletes like LeBron James and Patrick Mahomes. All of these people have worked hard to earn their success, the tech moguls working long hours to grow their businesses and the athletes working and conditioning from a young age to perfect their athleticism. We call what drives these people to keep going even when the going gets tough, *heart* or *passion*. To be successful, your heart must be in pursuit and passionate about the things you desire. You will encounter many challenges, some of which you will need to endure if you are passionate about getting what you want.

Professionals like technologists and athletes understand the importance of applying the process of development. Yet many leaders who God supposedly called do not know why God established His process, let alone have the desire to follow the process. The whole world—whether they realize it or not, must complete the process of development, cultivation, and the process of being sent forth.

If we look at Zuckerberg, who launched into Facebook when he was in his early twenties, we will see that he knew he had a gift. Zuckerberg understood that the world needed what God placed on the inside. So he stepped into it. Sure, he encountered some roadblocks, but he developed and grew along the way. Many are too afraid of failure and will never move forward in faith, and others are simply bound by the wrong leaders who are sucking the life out of them and not pushing them to propel into their divine purpose.

A Limitless Kingdom

There are no limitations in the Kingdom. Everything you will need, as a leader and child of God, is found in two places. Colossians 1:27 shows us the first, as it says, "Christ in you, the hope of glory." First and foremost, all that we will need, as the Scripture says, is in Christ. It is the power and authority of Jesus Christ that we can prevail. Secondly, as Luke 17:21 says, "The kingdom of God is within you." As born-again believers of Jesus Christ, we have the gift of the Holy Spirit of God, which avails us the privilege of having the Kingdom of Heaven within us.

Therefore, when you look to the world and anywhere outside of yourself, you are looking in the wrong place. You are supposed to look within yourself. Look to Christ who is in you. In addition, you are supposed to look at the Christ that is within other fellow believers. You should not look at them in the flesh, but look at the Spirit of God that is within them. You must discern and connect with those by the spirit. God wants us to discern who is of Him and His Kingdom and who is not. However, that is where the problem comes.

Most people, including what we call the church, do not know how to identify accurately the gifts that rest within themselves nor others. Thus, they do not know how to acknowledge spiritual leadership properly. Most people are confused, and society will attempt to put everybody within boxes and define godly spiritual leadership. Yet, when you are in the Kingdom, you will never fit the mold of man's box because there are no limits to your life, as there are no limitations in the Kingdom of Heaven.

The world always has limitations; the world functions in a way that automatically imputes limitations on people. Even those at the top of the pyramid have limitations. Everyone at the top is limited to what they can produce within themselves or those subjugated to them. Thus, most people cannot see God; quite frankly, most people do not adequately see themselves. Therefore, they can never see the world correctly. The real question is, if most people do not have a relationship with God — including some church folks, how will they see you? If they have a skewed perspective of God, themselves, and the world, then they will have a skewed perspective about you.

About 90 percent of the people within this world do not know each other, and the same percentage do not know you. Sadly, this is also true within the physical church. You can be a church member for a year or more, and the leadership will never recognize or know you. And if you are a prophet or called to other offices or have other spiritual gifts and your leader does not invest time to nurture your gifts and callings, then you must pay extreme attention. If this is the case for you, you are in the wrong place, and you are among the wrong people. Your spiritual leaders should identify your spiritual gifts and calling and provide a safe space to nurture what is inside you.

Who Is Holding Them Accountable?

In addition to providing a safe space where your gifts and callings can be nurtured and cultivated, leaders must hold you accountable while being held accountable. Where there is no accountability, you will find an unqualified or unfit leader. Unfit leaders do not have accountability to God, nor men, nor the people they govern. When encountering leaders who are void of accountability, it is a red flag: run!

God is sovereign and has established everything before the conception of the world. However, many play the role of god and choose to live however they want. Oddly enough, they think they can live however and expect God's results. This is impossible. If you are not connected with quality, qualified leadership, then you will become unqualified or disqualified. As a result, your life will be in a perpetual state of mediocracy. You will remain stagnant and stuck and in desperate need of a breakthrough. You will not have progress, nor will you produce fruit.

If you desire to grow and become all that God has destined for you, you must be connected to a qualified, quality spiritual leader. Unqualified and disqualified people are self-seeking and are not concerned about your soul. They are more concerned about what they can get from you and advancing their agenda.

Walk in the Fullness of Christ

The Bible says, "The heaven, even the heavens, are the Lord's; But the Earth He has given to the children of men" (Ps. 115:16). The Lord has given the responsibility of the land to man. We are to till the ground that God has given us. The only way to do so is to become Christ-like. If Christ knows how to rule and reign, then we must become more like Him, so we, too, can rule and reign. However, becoming Christ-like is rare because people do not want to sacrifice their temptations and surrender to Jesus. But God is dealing with that spirit of rebellion. God is dealing with the rebellious spirit to bring forth people who possess His heart, priorities, and agenda. These are they who must be the example to the people.

Although God is bringing forth His people who have His heart, we must understand that we have an adversary. Many things taking place that are not of God have been normalized. Far too often, issues have been tolerated and unattended. The Lord says, enough. No longer will we allow the roaming lion—our adversary, to creep into the places of worship, our nations, or our leaders. No longer will leaders remain petrified and reluctant to address the issues that are running rampant. The Lord has issued a clarion call and instructed us to do as the Bible says, to speak the truth with love.

If there is no truth, then there is no love. Where there is no love, God is not present. So if a leader is not honest and bold enough to sit others down and have a heart-to-heart, then there is an issue. Leaders must be able to lead with the expression of the Father's heart. For example, a leader must be willing and able to say, "Listen, I am sharing the revelation of the Father with you to build you up. My intentions are never to condemn you, castigate you, or throw stones at you. Instead, I am called to help deliver you, set you free, and get you on the right course so your life can be of quality and productivity, so you, too, can reproduce that productivity and blessing in others." Leaders must learn to lead appropriately.

So when we see a consistent, normalized dysfunction and a refusal to address common issues, there is a problem. Though the problem is within the houses of God, it does not originate at the House of God. Yes, the Bible says judgment starts at the House of God, but if a man does not know how to rule his own house *and affairs*, how will he take care of the House of God? (1 Tim. 3:5 *emphasis added*). You must get your home in order!

The Lord Will Teach His Children

I got saved right before I got married. I did not know anything. I was an ignorant believer, but I had the heart of God. I was sincere about walking with God. I said to God, "Show me how to be a husband. I need to be full for my wife." I knew I did not know how to be the husband my wife needed. I was not going to be perfect, but I also knew I was connected to God. As a result of my relationship with God, I knew our marriage would be to His glory. I knew I would do the job that would please God and be a blessing to my wife. Now, I have been married for over thirty-one years. I did not try to relate to my wife based on my feelings nor my opinion; I related to her according to how it would honor God.

I want God to be pleased with me. If I dishonor, mistreat, abuse, or abandon my wife, God is going to hold me accountable and responsible. I cannot treat my wife any kind of way. Although we are imperfect and do not say the right things, we will make sure we get it right and keep trusting God because He will hold us accountable.

We cannot represent God if we are not operating in order and excellence. I cannot represent God if my affairs, marriage, or children are not in order. The same can be said about my children, as they did not have a hypocritical father. They saw a man who loves God. I prayed to God, asking Him to give me wisdom and strength and to teach me how to be the father my children need. Now, my two daughters are grown and doing very well in their life. They are prosperous, blessed, and love God. My children were never forced or manipulated to love God. My children did not receive mixed messages, nor did they see religion on Sunday and failure throughout the week. My wife and I made sure our children saw God working in our lives. They witnessed the blessings of God and saw how God covered and provided for us. Therefore, they experienced the fullness of God and knew He was real.

People must be discipled, trained, and imparted with the revelation of the Scripture. Pure revelation will distinguish the true leaders, as they know how imperative it is to have their affairs intact and in God. It is the leaders with revelation who can bring forth teaching and training and impart revelation from the Word of God. These leaders are the ones who understand it is not about race or age, nor based on gender or ethnicity. It is about glorifying God and magnifying His name.

Additionally, God is doing away with stupidity. The Lord is removing the veil of stupidity from His people and creating them to be leaders after His heart who will feed His children with knowledge and understanding while giving them truth and love. God is replacing ignorant and incompetent leaders with those who will be an example and the proper ambassadors of His Kingdom.

Walking in Destiny

People want to feel appreciated, so many activities cater to the desires of men. Many people are doing various things, like starting businesses and ministries, especially young people. Many are launching new and creative things because God wires us to function as extraordinary people who invent and create. We were not wired to operate according to the systems of this world. God does not want us to mimic the likings of a manufacturing company where we present ourselves as prepackages from an assembly line of this world. God does not want us to fit the mold of living and doing life in a way that is tailored by this world. God created us for so much more. We were never made to fit the mold of society.

God created us to be unique and special. And He intentionally made us that way because we all bring something unique and different to the table. Ephesians 4:16 testifies to our uniqueness. Everyone has something to offer and has something to provide for the table. But most people do not bring anything to the table because they have not discovered what they have.

You will be stuck if you do not know what is in you. You must discover what has to be developed within you and go through the process of being equipped, cultivated, prepared, and deployed. If you do not tap into your potential and pursue the things of God, you will experience frustration. Most people live their lives frustrated, with low morale and no motivation, simply in hopelessness — the direct factors that cause people to live in bondage. Many are trapped in an unfulfilled state, which leads to hosts of crippling bondage.

Yet on the other side is fear. Most people will not move into their calling because it is unfamiliar. It is not what they are accustomed to nor based on society's standards or their family's traditions. But you must ask yourself, who will you serve? Will you serve God or man? Will you serve God or the devil? Serving God means that you are forsaking all and choosing to follow the will and leading of the Holy Spirit. You are making a definitive decision to say yes to the Lord. You must break free from the spirit of fear and thoughts of inadequacy so you can wholly walk into the person the Lord destined.

God has sent His Holy Spirit to endow us and impart His gifts and will unto us. We have the ability and capability to use what God has placed on the inside of us to influence people. But you must walk in faith even when it appears as if those you are called to are not receptive. As you continue to walk in the Lord and seek Him, know that the people God has assigned to your life are the ones into whom you are to pour what God has imparted.

Gift of God

At this point, I want to share a testimony about my mother. My mother was a phenomenal tailor. However, she did not attend tailoring, sewing, nor seamstress courses. She never went to college or a vocational school. Yet my mother could run circles around people who were skillfully trained in making clothes. When I pondered her inherent skills, the Holy Spirit began answering the question: where did she obtain her skills? She did not get her gifts by her lonesome, nor did she receive formal training. The only answer: they were a gift from God. It was God who gave her the skills of a seamstress and enabled her. It was the enablement and endowment of the Holy Spirit that caused her to be a master of her profession.

Likewise, UNC did not give the skill of basketball to Michael Jordan. Michael Jordan was already great before he went to UNC. The same is true for Tiger Woods; no person nor entity gave Tiger his skills and ability to play golf. Sure, they helped develop and cultivate Tiger Woods into the player he is. However, they did not give him the gift of being able to play golf. All the greats and those who are in your backyard received their anointing and gifts from the Lord. Sure, many attended college and received other forms of training, but the ultimate ability rests in their DNA. Everybody has their fingerprint without duplications.

God has gifted each a measure of a unique personality and divine enablement so that they can fulfill all that is required. Even more so, God has granted you a measure of grace and anointing to complete your call and purpose in life. However, it is your responsibility to seek what God has planted inside and position yourself within the proper environment for cultivation.

Notes

2

Lifestyle of Prayer

Spiritual Transactions

Transactions, whether spiritual or natural, are the things that cause a change or put change in motion. Transactions are a direct exchange of input and output. Spiritual and natural transactions always occur. When there is an exchange, there is a change taking place. When it comes to transactions, there is first a change that takes place. Next, there are transitions. Transitions are the process of the transaction. Transitioning is the actual process of change. Finally, there is transformation. Transition is the result of the change that initially took place. Transactions are constantly at play in the spiritual realm as in the natural realm. Therefore, we must pay keen attention to actions and reactions, as they involve spiritual transactions.

Because transactions are a direct exchange of input and output, what you put in will produce a change that will eventually create transition. Thus Galatians 6:7 will continuously be evident in our lives. We will always reap what we have sown. Spiritually speaking, many people tend to ask, "Why is this happening to me?" or "Why are bad things happening?" The answer: things will or will not happen if the right or wrong transactions are made.

When correct transactions are made, the transitional process will result in the proper and desired transformations. However, when wrong transactions occur, undesired transitions will occur, resulting in an unfavorable outcome. Therefore, we must no longer make bad, ungodly, evil, immoral, unethical, etc. transactions and then question the result. You will always sow what you reap. What you sow in the natural will manifest itself naturally and spiritually. What you sow spiritually, you will always reap naturally and spiritually.

Deny Thyself

Because we live in a perpetual state of transactions and sowing what we reap, we must understand the vitality of dying to ourselves so that we can surrender to the will of God. If we do not submit to the will of God, by default, we will reap worldly factors while being void of God's divinity within our lives. Should we desire to live ultimate quality lives, then we must note our biblical example and follow suit in the blueprint of God.

Jesus lived a life of self-denial and obedience to the Father to fulfill an objective to resurrect in life so that we may partake in His resurrection and receive His Holy Spirit. Luke 3:22 says, "And the Holy Spirit descended in bodily form like a dove upon Him." The Bible says, "The spirit of man is the candle of the Lord" (Prov. 20:27, KJV). The Spirit of God is the light in our hearts. When Jesus came out of the water, the Spirit came on him like a dove; we can compare this to John 3:5. To be "Born of water and of Spirit" is referring to spiritual awakening.

Spiritual reality is one thing, but spiritual activation, spiritual awakening, spiritual igniting is another. When the Holy Spirit awakens you, your spirit comes alive. Because the Holy Spirit is within you and has awakened your soul, The Holy Spirit can now lead your life. The Holy Spirit is present within you. It is the Spirit of God who is directing, leading, and convicting you to live Christ-like. Therefore, the Bible talks about being baptized in the Holy Spirit. The Holy Spirit must be present and apparent within our lives.

God wants us to understand that in this walk of life, we cannot operate in the power of the Spirit, experience the glory of His presence, nor walk in the demonstration of the Holy Spirit if we have not denied ourselves. Jesus revealed this truth as He ministered to Nicodemus. He said in John 3:6, "That which is born of the flesh is flesh, and that which is born of the Spirit is spirit." You cannot come into the Kingdom of God in the flesh. You must be ignited in your spirit, engulfed, and awakened while being led and governed by the Holy Spirit. That is the sign of Christ.

Jesus died, but Christ resurrected. The same thing applies to us. We live in death, but we live in life. In our flesh, we are mortal beings destined for death. However, in our Spirit, through Christ, we live. Yet many have not comprehended such truth. Thus, many people are not demonstrating the power of God nor manifesting His glory in life. Many have not partnered with Christ — The Resurrector and Life.

As we partner with Christ, The Resurrector, we must remember it is not only what we say that produces evidence of the resurrecting power that rests within us. Most importantly, it is our walk, our manifestation, and our demonstration that bears light to the light that is within us. Our action is evidence to people in darkness, including those not saved and those who are religious. We must be true ambassadors and representatives of Jesus Christ. Our actions must back our faith and the resurrecting power of Christ. Above all else, we must have a prayer life that expresses the true heart and intent of the Father.

The Model Prayer

Having a heart posture of prayer means we understand the magnitude of completely denying ourselves so Christ's glory can resurrect within us. It is when we surrender our will and desires that we walk in the power and lifestyle of prayer. We must understand that as believers, prayer is a powerful arsenal that God gave. Therefore, we must thoroughly rid ourselves of the matters of this world and seek the face of the Father.

God wants His children to be equipped with prayer. It is through prayer in which we can adequately intercede as leaders and true disciples of the Lord. Therefore, as leaders and members of the Body of Christ, we must identify with the structure and blueprint of prayer that Jesus administered. According to Matthew 6, we see the heart pattern and posture for prayer, and if we take a deeper look, we will notice that prayer is a normal part of our lives and a lifestyle for all believers. Here is our example and blueprint from Matthew 6:5-14 that Jesus displayed:

> And when you pray, you shall not be like the hypocrites. For they love to pray standing in the synagogues and on the corners of the streets, that they may be seen by men. Assuredly, I say to you, they have their reward. But you, when you pray, go into your room, and when you have shut your door, pray to your Father who is in the secret place; and your Father who sees in secret will reward you openly. And when you pray, do not use

vain repetitions as the heathen do. For they think that they will be heard for their many words.

Therefore, do not be like them. For your Father knows the things you have need of before you ask Him. In this manner, therefore, pray:

Our Father in heaven, Hallowed be Your name. Your kingdom come. Your will be done on earth as it is in heaven. Give us this day our daily bread. And forgive us our debts as we forgive our debtors. And do not lead us into temptation, but deliver us from the evil one. For Yours is the kingdom and the power and the glory forever. Amen.

Additionally, many are unaware that forgiveness is a vital component of prayer and bearing the heart of the Lord. Here is what Jesus spoke of as it pertains to prayer: "For if you forgive men their trespasses, your heavenly Father will also forgive you. But if you do not forgive men their trespasses, neither will your Father forgive your trespasses"(Matt. 6:14).

According to God, prayer should be as normal as breathing. Prayer is not about a moment or specific time or physical position. Instead, prayer is about remaining connected with God by the posture of our heart.

Prayers of Impartations

At this moment, through prayer, I want to impart the revelation, manifestation, and demonstration of the Kingdom of God.

Prayer for Freedom from Religious Strongholds

In the name of Jesus, I demolish and destroy the spirit of atheism, agnosticism, carnality, religion, family tradition, and worldly indoctrinations. God, they are destroying Your people. So in the name of Jesus, I impart revelation, manifestation, and the demonstration of God's Kingdom. Lord, let the revelation of your Kingdom manifest and be demonstrated in those who receive it.

Thank you, Jesus, for this profound revelation and teaching. I pray it will bless the receiver. I pray Your child will see a positive impact in their life due to them obeying and receiving Your Word. In the name of Jesus Christ, I thank you, Lord. I praise you. God, in Your Son Jesus's name, I pray. Hallelujah. Amen.

Prayer for Divine Leadership Connection

Father, I pray that You will clearly distinguish people. Lord, let us see and know who Your true spiritual leaders are in the modern day and times that we are living. Help us connect with the right leaders so our lives can flourish and we can awaken, activate and come alive for your glory. God, I pray that You allow us to connect with authentic leadership and disconnected from unqualified and disqualified leaders.

God, I pray that You expose every ill-equipped leader and help us identify how they are stumbling blocks in our walk and relationship with You. Lord, I pray that You allow us to see and perceive the spiritual leaders You have established.

Holy Spirit, help us to pray. Lord, allow us to seek You continuously and bless us with the gift of discernment so we can discern the wrong leaders. Lord, help us to operate according to Your will and for Your glory. In the name of Jesus, Lord help us to lead like You, Amen.

Notes

3

The Bible

God is reestablishing order and His priorities. First, He is dealing with leadership. He is establishing order within His administration and the foundational structure. God is reestablishing His divine order of what a Kingdom body of believers is supposed to look and how it is supposed to function. A key distinction of a true leader of Christ is the indication of a life built on prayer, study, and the meditation of the Word of God. Being intentional about sitting at the feet of Jesus is the catalyst to developing whole people and, ultimately, a whole and fully functioning Body of Christ.

God has always chosen His spiritual leaders to lead His people into righteousness and holiness. Not everybody is consumed with money and materialism. Some focus on the right priorities and are genuinely concerned about the souls of people being made whole and complete.

Spiritual leadership is a gift to the Body of Christ. Many people acknowledge or recognize different gifts, but they may not necessarily know what is in that gift. In other words, they identify with having the gift or recognize the gift based on the name or the package. However, God told me they are unaware of what is inside of the gift or package. They can identify it, relate to it, and receive it with gladness. However, they are more concerned about the package or having the gift, but not what is inside the package or the purpose of having the gift.

Soul Prosperity

When you think about a priority, you think about what should come first, second, third, and so on. Third John 2 says, "Beloved, I pray that you may prosper in all things and be in health, just as your soul prospers." The priority is soul prosperity. Next should be physical prosperity, which precedes financial or material prosperity. That is the order and will of God.

So the priority of a spiritual leader should be to ensure that your soul is prospering, blessed, and healthy and whole. The priority should not be getting you somewhere, nor should it be trying to teach you to obtain something natural. Natural or earthly matters are a part of the package; they are not the priority. The priority is the matter of the souls.

When the first church started in the book of Acts, the Apostle Paul said something very profound. In Acts 6:4, Apostle Paul said, "But we will give ourselves continually to prayer and to the ministry of the Word." Apostle Paul's sentiment deals specifically with the interior of the package, or in other words, the matters of the heart and soul. The priority and focus on spiritual leadership must be in prayer and the study and meditation of the Word of God. Jesus demonstrated supernaturally because of His time of prayer, meditation, and focus on the Word of God. The Word of God was His priority.

How do we know the Word of God is the priority? Because toward the end of Jesus's crucifixion, He said, "It is finished" (John 19:30). Jesus possessed the authority to make the settling verdict because He was the Word made of flesh. "It is finished," meant everything that the Bible exemplifies is a completed and finished work. Jesus finished the work in the flesh, but the Word of God is complete because the work of Jesus Christ has been fulfilled.

Where Is Your Heart?

You must ask yourself, are you more concerned about the package — the gift itself and the wrappings of the gift? Or are you more concerned about the actual gift and its contents? What concerns you the most? It should be what is in the package. If you do not unwrap the package, you cannot receive the benefit from the gift or use it for its intended purpose. All gifts from God are good. However, until the blessing is unwrapped, embraced, and used for its intended purpose, you will not receive its benefits.

The contents and what is inside a spiritual gift are most important. However, too many people are only concerned about the outside and the presentation of a spiritual gift. Many leaders within the Body of Christ are similar in this way as well. They care too much about presentation and are not focused on consecration.

A true spiritual leader is always concerned about what is on the inside of the gift, consecrating the heart. If we continue to examine 3 John 2, it says, we will understand that the priority first and foremost is prayer, study, and meditation on the Word. It is about souls demonstrating and living by the Word of God, the Kingdom of God. It is a holistic approach; it applies to every aspect of our lives.

Restore the Priority

The priority is the wholeness of our soul and our body. As we can see today, there is not enough emphasis or demonstration on a life of prayer, study, and meditation on the Word. Ultimately, there is no emphasis on people becoming whole. The priority must be refocused on what God says leaders should prioritize, which entails being whole and bearing the capacity to teach and lead people into their wholeness.

Often, you will hear people talk about *shifts*. The term *shift* is more focused on social and natural things shifting. However, Jesus is more concerned about us becoming instead of us shifting. We must become whole before we can shift. We become whole by becoming more like Jesus. The priority and focus, especially for spiritual leaders, should be to lead, train, and develop people to become more like Christ. To be Christ-like means that the sinful nature, all things that stand between Jesus and us, must be addressed. To become whole is to become like Christ.

The emphasis is becoming more Christ-like. When we hear prophetic words and teachings, often, it revolves around going somewhere and getting something such as success and material things. However, most people's souls are broken and have voids; here lies the major problem. We need more leaders who are genuine about cultivating souls into wholeness.

God wants people to be as whole as possible before getting married and before entering into serious relationships and ministry. If you do these things without becoming whole, especially within marriage, issues will arise. Most often, in marriages, if the matters of the heart nor wholeness are addressed, you will have two broken people. In the end, you will have each person feeding off the other, trying to obtain wholeness. Such is not God's will. Whether dealing with marriage, ministry, or other forms of relationships, God wants His people whole.

In Scriptures, whenever Jesus dealt with somebody, even in healing, deliverance, and salvation, the whole idea was for that person to be made whole. Jesus's prime focus was not riches nor status quo, but a person's wholeness. What good is life if our soul is not whole? What good is it to chase money, fame, success, climbing up the corporate ladder, or running our business if our soul is broken?

You must ask yourself, "Is my leader capable, responsible, and focused on the priority of my soul being whole?" Your spiritual leaders have a direct correlation with the wholeness of your soul. Therefore, you must ensure your leaders are leading with the intention of bearing and reproducing wholeness.

Mind of Christ

The beginning stages of wholeness, spiritual growth, and becoming transformed into the image and likeness of Christ is to be transformed by the renewing of your mind. Being transformed by the renewing of our minds is putting on the mind of Christ (Rom. 12:2 & Phil. 2:5). God does not want us to think like ourselves. God wants us to have His mind. Romans 12:2 says, "Be transformed by the renewing of your mind."

God's sole purpose is for us to come into wholeness by a work of the Spirit. Not to be successful. However, there is nothing wrong with being successful. Yet, we must note, being prosperous is a byproduct of the things of Christ; it is not God's priority.

The Word of God says, "Seek first the kingdom of God and His righteousness, and all these things shall be added to you"(Matt. 6:33). Our entire being must be in right standing and in the process of transforming into the image and likeness of Christ. As we continue to become more Christ-like and seek God's Kingdom, then all will be added unto us. God naturally wants to bless His children with their hearts' desires. The Word of God says, "Delight yourself also in the Lord, And He shall give you the desires of your heart" (Ps. 37:4). God has no problem blessing us. However, too many people are chasing after blessings.

When you are whole or in the process of becoming whole and transformed into the image of Christ, you do not have to chase anything. Everything that is assigned to your name will chase after you. It will find you. "Things are going to happen so fast your head will swim, one thing fast on the heels of the other. You won't be able to keep up. Everything will be happening at once—and everywhere you look, blessings!" (Amos 9:13, MSG)

Demonstration of God

You must be able to speak the heart and mind of God in any situation. You must demonstrate. The Bible says that signs confirm God's word (see Mark 16:20). So, if you witness words and do not produce confirmation, then it is not God.

Words are a great thing; we know words are powerful, but words in themselves are nothing. Thus, God talks about words being Idle (see Matt. 12:36). Your words can produce life or death. God talks about how every man will account for every idle word (see Matt. 12:36). You must ask, can your words bring results, confirmation, or produce signs? We need demonstration.

Demonstration results in a change and provides answers and solutions to people's and the world's problems. If you cannot solve problems, you will be irrelevant to the church and those you are called to help. You must demonstrate the ability to solve problems and provide solutions. We are created to solve problems. Jesus, in all His ways, solved problems.

Jesus solved problems by speaking and doing as God led. He never spoke idle words. In fact, the people were amazed at what He said because Jesus spoke what God revealed to Him. He did not speak of His own accord nor from what He felt nor His experiences. Jesus never spoke from His flesh. Jesus always spoke as God gave Him utterance and revelation.

After Jesus declared what thus saith the Lord, He demonstrated. Your words alone are not enough, and neither are your leaders. Therefore, most people look at the church and think it is a joke. All they hear is talk; they do not see demonstration, manifestation, fruit, nor problems being solved.

Our Great Demonstrator

Jesus is our Greatest Demonstrator. Jesus Christ told John He must be baptized in water. Jesus set the precedence for what this life is all about. His posture said, "It is not only by My Word, but I must also demonstrate." Jesus knew He was to be seen as someone regular while walking the earth. Jesus knew the power of His demonstration. Thus, He embodied His calling and demonstrated How we are to walk in His footsteps.

I hope many people understand the significance of the baptism of water and the baptism of the Holy Ghost. We must have both in our life. Additionally, there must be a constant acknowledgment of what it is to die to self, which is a crucified life. Unfortunately, many people wear crosses around their necks but do not understand the full magnitude of what that cross symbolizes.

That cross of Jesus Christ is about living a sacrificial death-to-life experience. We are supposed to live a life crucified with Christ and resurrected in Him; that is Jesus the Christ. Jesus is the man Jesus. The man who died is the man who suffered. Jesus lived the life of death and is now Christ, the resurrected Messiah, the Anointed One who lived a life of glory and God in the flesh. Christ has the power of life and lived a life of demonstration, glory, and the power of God. Both elements must simultaneously be at work to live. You cannot have the power of Christ without the death of Jesus. You cannot have the death of Jesus without the power of Christ. Like Jesus, you must die to your flesh so you can represent and demonstrate the power of Jesus Christ within your life.

Balancing Wholeness

Imagine having a lifestyle devoted to praying, fasting, and meditating on the Word of God. You will begin to walk and live from the revelation of the Holy Spirit, and as a result, you will operate with demonstration. Because Jesus knew the importance of consecration, He was able to walk in the manifestation of the Holy Spirit. Unfortunately, today, we are missing a consecrated lifestyle. We have become so numb with words and have failed to demonstrate power and authority. The Bible says, "For the Kingdom of God is not in word but in power"(1 Cor. 4:20).

Prayer and the Word of God grant you the authority to operate with revelation and demonstration. It is not what is in the package, how it is wrapped, what it looks like, or how it presents itself. But it is the demonstration that matters. We must gather all that God gave and apply it to our lives and walk, but with balance. Yes, we have the Word of God, but words by themselves will not do. We can easily say a word, but our actions must measure up to our declaration. We need demonstration. Yes, we can demonstrate the power of God, but do we have the Word in us? We need both the Word of God and the demonstration of power flowing through us. The two must always work hand-in-hand.

Everything about God exudes balance. A whole person walking in holiness will understand that walking with God is in balance. Walking in balance is walking in faith and wisdom. You have your eyes open; your spiritual senses are sharp, alert, and attentive. You are walking in discernment and not in fear. You walk circumspectly and sensitive to the spiritual climate. Most importantly, you are demonstrating the power of God because you are spiritually aware of the time and season

Notes

4

Discipleship

It is time to assess your driving force. Does your flesh, the soulish realm, drive you, or does the Holy Spirit lead you? Too often, people are enticed by the lust of the eye and are drawn to spiritual leaders based on what is pleasing to their eyes and other fleshly senses. However, If you allow your flesh and your emotions to connect with leaders who are unfit and more concerned about worldly matters over God's will, then that places you in jeopardy of following in their footsteps.

Even more so, if the leaders you are connected to are not quality, then the gifts and purposes that God has placed on the inside of you will lay dormant. It is God's will that you use all gifts and utilize the anointing He has given you. Therefore, God is greatly concerned about who you are connected to spiritually. The Lord knows that some leaders place hindering blocks on the fruition of you being used to capacity because of their inhibitions. Also, just as a leader can hinder you due to their issues, the right leader can cultivate and catapult you into your destiny.

You must understand my argument. I am not telling you to leave your church nor disregard your home church pastor. I am urging you to get plugged into the right leadership, because it is not about going to church. It is more important to God that you are rightly aligned with the right leaders. Even more so, you must be aware because some leaders are idolized, and some control others.

Admittedly, many people do not mind being controlled because that takes away their responsibility and accountability. A true leader is responsible to God and is responsible and accountable to those under their leadership. Many people do not understand the nature of *responsibility* and *accountability* because the church is predominately about pumping people up to make them *feel good*. Some leaders are more concerned with creating an ambiance, an atmosphere, and a setting that makes people feel good about coming to church. Unfortunately, those churches are not focused on equipping people nor activating people. If those churches 'hearts' desires are not about people coming into the fullness of their purpose and identity, then you must ask yourself, are their intentions selfish ambitions, or do they desire to fulfill the mandate of the Kingdom of Heaven?

God's Ultimate Will for Leadership

Despite inadequate leadership, the Lord expects everyone to submit to leadership. No matter who you are, what level you are on, now or later, leadership is mandatory. There must always be leadership. In fact, the first level or first experience of leadership that we all had were our parents or guardians. Now, whether they are good or bad or whatever the case may be, parents are our God-given authority and leader. However, the challenge is paralleling that or tying it to spiritual leadership, which should be the most influential leaders in our lives journey. Sadly, finding exemplary leadership is an enormous challenge. Too many people have experienced leadership with unqualified or disqualified leaders.

Most people are accustomed, conditioned, and brainwashed into accepting and tolerating an idea or experience they have with their leaders. Many have accepted leadership for the sake of someone standing in a man-made role. Just because a person is in a leadership position does not mean they are a leader, nor does it mean they are a qualified leader. You cannot arbitrarily become a leader. You must be called and sent by God.

Leadership is not about receiving attention or status. Leadership is about responsibility and accountability. Leaders are to set a higher standard while simultaneously being held to a higher degree. According to Scripture, God assigns leaders to be servants. Also, leadership must influence people into knowing God while encouraging people to be like God. Leaders are supposed to be ambassadors of God on the Earth.

The Five-Fold Ministers

In Ephesians 4, God gave a detailed description of His body of leaders, also known as His *five-fold ministers*. Throughout church history, specifically in a religious denomination setting, people have freely embraced and accepted reverends, pastors, and bishops as the top of their leadership chain. On the contrary, apostles, prophets, evangelists, and teachers are vastly rejected.

If leaders continue to reject the full five-fold ministers, they will be deficient and lacking the ability to lead God's people into becoming fully activated and awakened. If leaders are not adequately joined with other leaders, then voids are created. There will be deficiencies and errors within the church system because God gave us a body of leaders who are supposed to be fully unified and functioning. When we are not properly joined as a body of believers, we are not operating to the total capacity that God has prescribed. We must have exemplary people who can sufficiently lead by showing and telling. We need real ambassadors who will represent Christ and the fullness of who He is and His will for humanity.

Who Are You Connected To?

Because it takes the Word of God and the Holy Spirit to activate a believer fully, you must govern who ministers the Word of God to you. You must be connected to exceptional spiritual leadership. Here is why: Let us say we are power cords to an appliance that requires power to work. This appliance has a light that must be activated, and the power cord (us) must be connected to a wall socket to activate that light. However, a wall socket (spiritual leaders) is not the power source. The wall socket is the conduit to the Power Source (God). Spiritual leaders serve as a conduit to the Power Source of our lives.

We must remain connected. Some refuse to be plugged into the conduit, which is connected to the Power. Others are plugged into the conduit, but the conduit is not connected to the Source of Power. If you are plugged into the conduit, your spiritual leadership, but there is no power flowing, no activation or awakening, then that conduit is unfit.

Sadly, most people do not have the spiritual revelation, basic spiritual knowledge, and logic to understand God's mandate for His saints to remain connected to a conduit. God has never done anything on this earth without a person. From Genesis to Revelation, God has raised spiritual leaders to lead His people. There were many leaders whom God appointed to lead His people toward blessings, prosperity, promises, victory, and His anointing. You must be connected to a suitable conduit. No, the conduit is not the Source. However, your leader is an essential element in the process. They are the connector that aligns your path to the Source of life.

On the contrary, a lot of people have a single conduit. They are only plugged into one person, one source. However, being connected to one conduit poses many issues. There is no way you can meet the conditions God prescribed by Scripture if you are only connected to one leader. Hebrews 10:25 tells us not to forsake assembling ourselves but to exhort one another. It is important to know that as believers, it is okay to receive impartation from other leaders besides your pastor. Some believe that the pastor of their home church is sufficient and additional leadership guidance is not a requirement. However, when God released the mantles of the five-fold ministry, He knew that each member would rely on the others. You will always need the fullness of the Body of Christ. Never subscribe to the notion that you do not need others who are in the faith to uphold and to uplift you.

Identify the Type of Connection

Understanding that you must be connected to a conduit of excellence is one thing. However, knowing how to identify that you have been appropriately knitted is another. Here are a few telltale signs that you have made a connection with a suitable conduit.

1. Your leader has a genuine relationship with the Power Source — God.

2. Your leader's words speak to your spirit and convict you into improving your life.
3. Your leaders must be connected to other spiritual leaders who are connected to the source of Power.

When you are rightly connected to the proper leadership, you will walk in the fullness of who God has created you to be. Adequate leadership ensures that you are fully awakened and activated, and utilized to your full potential.

The Ultimate Purpose

The objective is to ensure you are connected to the proper conduit and adequate spiritual leadership. If you do not affiliate with exemplary spiritual leaders, then you are in trouble. Not only are you in danger, but you are going to stay in a compromising situation until you are connected to someone who can make sure you are fully activated in the Lord.

When we say *trouble awaits*, it is not only speaking to the dangers of being under inadequate spiritual leadership. Trouble also awaits because many spiritual leaders are in positions for the wrong reasons. A lot of people want to be the boss and want attention. However, a true leader, according to Scripture, is the greatest servant. True leaders are not concerned about being served, but serving (see Matt. 20:28). God-ordained leaders are more concerned about following the Father's ways than following the masses (see Luke 2:49).

When you have a leader who serves as unto the Lord, it is their priority to ensure your spiritual gifts are being stirred and activated so God can use you as He sees fit (see 2 Tim. 1:6). Additionally and certainly among many more, true leaders know the importance of praying and interceding on behalf of the saints (see Luke 22:31-32). Therefore, we have many ill-prepared and unequipped leaders because they have not desired the better things of God, nor are they operating according to the heart of Jesus.

Remember, when you have a true leader, you will always experience the spirit of servanthood, as that will be the norm. Servitude will be the common factor that will stand out to you. You will recognize that although a person is your leader and has an essential role in your life, the consistent thing you will always feel and experience is servanthood. Leaders know that they are accountable to God and are responsible for leading you as if they are serving unto the Lord (see Eph. 6:7).

The Process of a Leader

Jesus facilitated a weeding-out process. He said, "If anyone does not drink of My blood and eat of My flesh, he is not worthy of Me. And many walked away from Him. Then He turned to those close to Him and said, are you going to leave Me too?" (See, John 6:51-57). Jesus went through the weed-out process. But the church today is trying to go through the blow-up process. A lot of churches are trying to become famous and well-known. Materialism means nothing.

Sadly, many go to church, whether they grew up in church or not, and remain the same. Their personal lives have not been impacted for the better. Many stories are the same. In one scenario, we have mama, who is not married or divorced two or three times. On the other hand, we have families where the dad is not present. But we go to church. We should not be spiritual church members and continuously experience struggle, poverty, and not making progress in life. Where is the joy in hugging a pew and keeping it warm? There is no peace nor fruitfulness beyond the four walls of a church. That is a problem that must be changed.

We should not go to church for a high or to receive a feel-good message. We go to church to medicate our dysfunctional problems for a couple of hours, and sometimes all day. However, when we go home, nothing has changed. Everything stays the same. And we wonder why the youth grow up and want to become rappers, entertainers, and athletes of the world and not give honor to God for their gifts.

The hypocrisy within religion and their environments has caused a disdain for God. Unfortunately, it started at home. However, many have also witnessed this hypocrisy in their community. They saw how religion produced dysfunction, disunity, destruction, and defeat. So naturally, many individuals want nothing to do with God nor church folks. If these young people saw prosperity, breakthrough, and the presence of God in their homes and their environments, they would know how to live a life that is pleasing to God.

This life is about drawing the multitudes. It is not about blowing up and having followers, which is the devil's motive. Making disciples is about teaching people how to love God with all their hearts. It is about being an example of Christ's likeness to this world while becoming carriers of the glory of God. We must become examples of fruitfulness. You can only exemplify these traits when you know and follow God. As a result, people are going to take notice of your God. When you walk in the fullness of Christ, you become a conduit to His blessing and point all the attention to God.

Spiritual leaders, you must reflect Christ. When people see you, they should see Jesus. When people hear you talk, they should hear Jesus. When people are around you, the presence they encounter should be the presence of the Lord. It should not be religion or hypocrisy. I implore you, leaders, to become a true disciple of Jesus Christ and follow in His footsteps.

Discovery, Development, and Deployment

God must raise people who can articulate spiritual revelation and give an accurate spiritual visual to settle in the hearts and minds of the people. Spiritual visuals must be visual representations of spiritual leadership. *Spiritual leadership,* explained in Ephesians 4:12, is "for the equipping of the saints for the work of ministry, for the edifying of the body of Christ."

Individuals must have spiritual leadership in their lives and the areas concerning the discovery, development, and deployment of individuals and their gifts and callings from God. As told by Dr. Myles Monroe, the greatest treasures of humanity are found in graveyards. There are untapped and unutilized gifts, skills, and ideas that God has placed in people. Most people live their entire lives without discovering qualities about themselves.

A genuinely qualified leader is the conduit to help people discover, develop, and deploy what is within them. There should not be graveyards full of untapped potential. However, most people are not connected to a suitable conduit, resulting in a life of frustration and the inability to become all that God has purposed.

Most people live unfulfilled and according to what they have been programmed and conditioned to believe in man's perspective of life. Too many people spend their entire lives thinking life is about getting something or going somewhere instead of focusing on becoming. When you become, what God has placed on the inside of you flows out of you naturally. Therefore, the discovery, development, and deployment of gifts are supposed to be something natural and normal. When we strain, press, push, and make all human efforts to try to get somewhere and get something and make something happen, we will encounter people who have low morale and no satisfaction or fulfillment in life. They have focused their lives around doing and getting instead of growing and becoming the person God designed.

The Bible says We have this treasure in earthen vessels that the excellence of the power may be of God and not of us (2 Cor. 4:7). So there are treasures that work by the power of God. And every born-again individual must be released first to discover themselves, then develop into what God destined, and finally, get activated and released/deployed. Every born-again believer must be set forth so the world can benefit from what is inside of them. Thus, the Bible says, gifts and calling are without repentance (Rom. 11:29, KJV). They are gifts and callings or, in other words, assignments. When God gives us gifts and callings, He will never take them back. Therefore, every believer must go through the process of discovery, development, and deployment.

There is a reason everyone is born into this world, but most people never discover why. Most people never had qualified leadership in their lives to help them unveil their gifts or calling, nor undergo the process of unearthing their potential. In other words, they've never had someone pull it out of them and allow it to flow. The blanket must be taken off, the veil must be removed, and the scales must fall so they can see what is truly in them. The treasure must be discovered. The proper spiritual leadership will possess the capabilities to equip you and assist you into becoming.

And I will give you shepherds according to My heart, who will feed you with knowledge and understanding (Jer. 3:15). The nature of spiritual leadership is possessing the heart of the Father. Leaders must know or have an inclination of what God has placed inside of the believer they are stewarding. Leaders must contain the knowledge, wisdom, and understanding to help believers unearth their God-given gifts and callings. Once a leader obtains insight into what is inside a believer, they must take the time and cultivate what is inside them so that God can wholly use that individual for His work in ministry. Leaders should never "hold" onto a servant, child of God, with fear of losing them or losing their control over them. Real spiritual leaders release God's children for the purposes for which God called them.

Cultivating Leaders

First Timothy 1 talks about how Apostle Paul was Fathering Timothy with his assignments and his gifts. Paul spoke of Timothy coming forth in who God called him to be and referenced things prophesied to him. Apostle Paul understood the mandate over Timothy's life and followed suit with the urgency of ensuring Timothy was discovered, developed, and deployed for the glory of God and the advancement of God's kingdom.

What has been prophesied about you? Do you know what God has placed on the inside? God wants what He has placed on the inside of you to come forward. God wants to reveal your treasure and your calling. One reason God wants to reveal what has been placed on the inside of you is because of prophecy. When a God-ordained prophetic word has been released over an individual, God will ensure that His word comes to pass, as His Words will not return to Him void (see Isa. 55:11).

Apostle Paul emphasized that he was not the first person who spoke into Timothy's life to identify his gifts and calling. It was prophesied to him before Paul referenced that fact. However, it took Paul, a qualified leader, to birth forth the development and the discovery of Timothy, which ultimately led to his deployment.

When you have the proper leadership, your life is impacted for the better. The right leader can pull out what God created you for, activate you, and bring forth life to the dry areas of your life. It will require a person qualified and capable of bringing forth the seeds God placed within.

Throughout first and second Timothy, Paul worked on the life of Timothy to prepare him, equip him, and cultivate him for his assignment and calling. God called Timothy to be an apostle, and it was imperative that Timothy was trained by an apostle—Paul.

Many believe they need to meet specific stipulations to be used by God. Sadly, the enemy and unfit leaders have manipulated the minds of believers. The motive was to persuade the believer to think they must obtain many accolades rather than hearing from God and being properly aligned. However, it is not to say that you do not need development. You must be developed to walk into maturity.

Some people's assignment requires their maturity process to be quicker than others. Sometimes, what God wills to do in one person will come to fruition sooner than in another. If we are not careful, we can view someone's expedited process as a means for competition. However, it is no competition; it is a process set by God. It is never about superseding anyone. Yet that is where most problems lie, especially with the younger generation. Many believe they must get somewhere quick and bypass the masses. God never said that things about our lives would be quick. There will be a process. No matter who we are, our calling and gifts must be developed. There must be a process of equipping, developing, and teaching. We must be trained for what is ahead of us. Most importantly, we must have the right leaders who are connected and a conduit to the Power Source.

Notes

5

The Church

Some people possess the false notion that you can have a personal relationship with God on your own. They believe you do not need church and can do whatever you choose. That mindset is unbiblical. The Bible says, "Not forsaking the assembling of ourselves together, as *is* the manner of some, but exhorting *one another*, and so much the more as you see the Day approaching" (Heb. 10:25). You must be connected. More importantly, you must be in proper connection.

Qualified and quality leadership is a jewel. It is a diamond in the rough, unique and different. Qualified and quality leaders have an aura and a persona about them. They have a God-given humility, grace, and confidence. Qualified and quality leaders can produce God-like traits because they are not in competition with anyone. They are not trying to compare themselves nor act like anyone. Quality leaders always want to be who God created and called them to be.

Church and the Family Nucleus

God intended for the church and the family unit to be the first spiritual leaders in an individual's life. Church and family are supposed to be the first demonstration of God and how one lives their life. So, my question is, are you experiencing a quality life from the people you are connected with and follow? You must experience quality, growth, and improvement from the leaders who are leading you.

Sadly, because the church and this culture are very shallow, most people see leadership based on superficial things. People look for the icing rather than the cake. People are more concerned about the gifts of individuals as opposed to the fruit. Everybody has gifts. The Bible says, "For the gifts and calling of God *are* without repentance"(Rom. 11:29, KJV). Therefore, we should not lust after gifts. Instead, we ought to look for the function and fruit. If you do not see spiritual function, spiritual progress, spiritual productivity, spiritual effectiveness, nor spiritual efficiency, then you have unqualified or disqualified leadership.

Most people will not tell you the truth, and many are not ready to hear the real and the raw. Someone once said, "Many people are just looking for the truth." As I listened, I almost agreed. However, the Holy Spirit reminded me of things that I have experienced and witnessed. The Holy Spirit's reminder showed me that her statement was false. People are not looking for truth. People are looking for what they are accustomed to or what they want. They are looking for an experience that is familiar and comfortable. People are not looking for what challenges them to evolve, grow, or go higher.

To improve the quality of your life, you must be challenged, corrected, trained, and developed. You cannot improve the quality of your life unless you have qualified and quality leaders who will nurture and cultivate you into an improved lifestyle. In the times that we live in, you will see more of the demise of many because they will not know how to identify, recognize, and align themselves with qualified, quality leadership.

The distinctions between the two types of leaders will be clear and will become more apparent. There will be no gray areas. Nearly everyone will be able to discern and rightly divide God-ordained leaders and unfit and unqualified leaders. So you must remain connected properly. If you are yoked with unqualified and unfit leaders, what category or position in life will that place you?

Heart of God

Currently, we have many people leading within the Body of Christ. However, the real question remains, do these leaders have the heart of God? According to Jeremiah 3:15, the Lord tells us that He will give us shepherds according to *His* heart, who will feed *us* with knowledge and understanding. The majority of leaders today are not leading from the heart of the Father. Today, many leaders within the Body of Christ are not leading effectively, proficiently, and relevantly. The bottom line: too many leaders today are either unqualified or disqualified to lead. Sadly, the stains of improper leadership within the Body of Christ are worn for all to see.

Both believers and nonbelievers of Jesus Christ are fully aware of how poorly most of God's children have misrepresented His Son, Jesus. In turn, it has left a bad taste in the mouths of so many nonbelievers. Therefore, many individuals are not receptive to the things about Jesus Christ and His Kingdom. We lack true sons and disciples of Jesus.

The lack of pure spiritual leadership representation has impacted how we function as churches and ministries and how we have been commanded to govern and function in this world. Thus, the Body of Christ is divided, dysfunctional, and filled with false doctrine and confusion. For these reasons, God is doing new work. God is positioning the proper spiritual leadership to win people and gather people the right way. God wants us to be a fully functioning, unified, and fruitful Body. We must be whole to win souls and bring them out of this world's systems, out of spiritual darkness, and into the marvelous light of Jesus Christ. We are mandated to gather souls before Jesus returns.

Therefore, we need the right leaders who are God-ordained leaders and not the people's leaders. We need qualified spiritual leaders at the forefront, leading the right way. And in return, the unqualified and disqualified leaders must be removed. They must go now!

Partner with Christ

The Body of Christ must understand that there are essential elements. We must have spiritual leaders who have the heart of God, spiritual knowledge, spiritual wisdom, and spiritual comprehension. Not only does the Word of God tell us that we need to have such leaders, but also that we must know the spirit that is behind the lifestyle and words that are preached, taught, and exemplified. We must test and discern the spirits that are motivating those who watch over us.

God's spiritual leaders speak into the lives of people, our spirits, and our souls, which impacts our entire lives. Also, God's leaders possess the spiritual authority and legal rights to change the spiritual dynamics of our nations. Therefore, to ensure what is being said contains the right spirit and produces the proper results, leaders must have God's heart, the Spirit of knowledge, and the Spirit of understanding to communicate, convey, and impart the heart of God into those they are leading.

We must know that God never intended the leadership roles to be apart from Him. God gave all, especially leaders, the anointing, power, and spiritual know-how to fulfill their roles and mandates. God's true leaders are equipped with revelation and wisdom and can effectively lead people in the direction God wants them to go. God's true leaders understand that their path will never be persuaded or persuade others to follow in the footsteps where many have strayed.

However, our major problem lies within training. The only way a leader can truly lead from the heart of God is if they are trained and processed by God. Many have not been trained, nor have they been led or guided by the Spirit of God. Some have not been perfected and equipped with the necessary tools to function within a team and the Body. Many leaders are not raised by God.

During my time in the military, I learned a crucial facet of being a good leader. Great leaders are, first and foremost, good followers. Should you become a good leader, you must have a blueprint and an example of what it means to lead. Who are you following? You are supposed to develop and grow into your role and function. You must be equipped to become who God called you to be, which requires proper and adequate training. Now, in addition to developing into a leader, we have natural-born leaders who lead instinctively. Yet whichever category you fall into, you must be equipped. Therefore, leader of the living God, you must be trained and processed.

Greater Purpose

It takes a certain kind of leader to usher in the fruition of God's will. Thus, as highlighted in Ephesians 4:11-12, God Himself called *some* apostles, some prophets, and some pastors and teachers. God called His select few to equip the saints for the work of ministry and edification and to come into the unity of faith and knowledge. Spiritual leaders are responsible to individuals within the Body while using their Biblical perspective and insight to impact the nation.

As you read in Ephesians 4:11-12, God not only called pastors, prophets, evangelists, etc. God also called all operating members within the five-fold ministry to fulfill His works and plans. As a leader, you are connected to a bigger mission that far outweighs your mandate. Therefore, leaders must cohesively work as a team while utilizing all skill sets, purposes, and giftings. Sadly, many individuals and leaders have neglected their responsibilities of fulfilling their leadership role within a team format.

Succession Plan

The perfect Biblical example of a leader being trained before stepping into the fullness of their position is Elisha. Elisha spent years following and being mentored by Elijah. And at the appointed time, Elisha received an impartation and a double portion of the work and ministry that Elijah fulfilled. Today, standards and protocols have not changed.

Impartation and succession plans are implanted to ensure that if a leader is retiring or involuntarily displaced or an unexpected life situation arises, someone is ready to fulfill the role and tasks at hand. God's mission and objectives will continue. Therefore, God will use people to lead His people so His mandate can be fulfilled.

God releases emerging leaders who have followed in the footsteps of one of His generals, front liners, or a previous leader. As we saw with Elijah and Elisha, God will ensure there are succession plans so that the quality and skills of one leader are passed down to the next. There will always be someone at the right time, the right season, and the perfect dispensation to be a leader.

We must understand that God-filled, quality, anointed leaders are needed. Apart from our purpose and vision, God has a mandate for all. The Lord desires that we go into all the world, make disciples of all nations (Matt. 28:19). God's sole and sovereign intent is for all to come out of the world, receive Jesus Christ as their Lord and Savior, and walk and operate in His Kingdom. Therefore, as a leader, God ultimately called you to fulfill His mandate of leading souls to salvation and the Kingdom of Heaven.

Peculiar People

Many people in the church will be surprised by the type of leaders emerging at the forefront. The church is going to have a more challenging time receiving them than the world. Many problems in this world need solutions. However, the root problem is the church. The issue lies within religion, tradition, and the brainwashing of tradition and religion. When the issues are prevalent, it creates a veil that blocks the world from receiving leaders that God has commissioned.

Because of the lack of proper and authentic representation, the world wants nothing to do with religion, tradition, and God. We must exemplify ourselves as true believers and God-ordained leaders. Yet the church is accustomed to accepting and normalizing unqualified and disqualified leaders. But God has other plans. He is breaking the mold of what we call normalcy.

There will be some leaders that will be relevant and needed. These individuals are what we call the "generals." The transition that is happening with the evolution and announcement of emerging and new leaders will only consist of a few leaders. Ephesians 4:11 says, "And He Himself gave some." The keyword is "some." So, if the Word of God says "some," why do we have so many leaders?

Simply put, people are self-appointed or appointed by people. However, few have been chosen. A person that walks as a leader and demonstrates the Kingdom is somebody that is anointed and ordained by God. Many people are functioning in the capacity of what we call leadership but are not leaders. They have not been appointed nor called by God. Thus we have a lack of equality and excellence in the church. In addition, there is a lack of quality in the people that are following these self-appointed leaders.

Qualified vs. Unqualified

You must discern unqualified or disqualified leaders, and you must know what it means to be qualified by God, not by the world's standards. The only way a person can live a quality life and produce or replicate quality is by being qualified to do so. Unfortunately, many people are not living quality lives—according to God's standards, because they have been connected to unqualified or disqualified people.

God anoints and chooses the people He wants to be His leaders. When God calls someone into a form of ministry for leadership, He qualifies them. However, the process looks different for everyone; it is not the same. Nonetheless, many people struggle with the process of becoming a leader. Most believe that to be qualified and used by God, you must measure up to worldly standards, which is inaccurate. If you look at the Biblical leaders whom God used, you will notice their process varied across the board.

Today, you will notice a few categories of leadership. In one category, you have leaders called by God and operating to their utmost and God-given purpose. Next, are those called and developed by God but have disqualified themselves from being used by God. Lastly, many people who God never qualified step into leadership positions. So that makes them unqualified. It is critical that as a leader, you are allowing God to fully process you, train you, and release you into your call of leadership and ministry. Even more, you must constantly consult God and seek Him for guidance and direction.

God in Us

A huge aspect of being a leader is showing others what you see. You must embrace and receive what you see so others can see it for themselves. If the people behind you do not embrace the objective or vision for themselves, you are not doing an adequate job as a leader. You, as a leader, must know how to show the people what you are seeing. If they do not see your vision, they cannot go where you are trying to take them.

God wants the world to see a reflection of himself through His disciples and His leaders. If people see God in others, lives will be transformed. However, the only way we can effectively see God in others is if the Word of God is being demonstrated.

If people see us doing what we say, preach, and teach, they will want to do what we are doing. Yet when they do not see proper representation, there is nothing attractive because they do not have a solid indication of who Christ is. The Bible says, "For the kingdom of

God *is* not in word but in power" (1 Cor. 4:20). Therefore, they must see a demonstration. People must see us in action.

You Must Choose

Jesus said He gave milk to those who are immature, who could not handle strong meat (see Heb. 5:13-14). Strong meat is for those who are mature or hungry. Are you hungry enough to eat strong meat? Or do you still want to suck on a pacifier or drink Similac? You must choose. Who will you associate with? Are you going to settle and accept mediocre leaders? Or will you allow God to place you among good leaders from whom you can grow and expand?

Understand this: by your association, you receive impartation. If you associate with unqualified and disqualified leaders, you will receive an impartation of being incompetent. However, if you associate with a qualified leader, you will receive an impartation of being qualified, which will cause you to be a qualified and of quality in the eyes of God. Choose wisely.

Notes

6

The Kingdom of God

The Kingdom of God

Many people do not have a clear understanding of the Kingdom of God. Most people have a natural concept of a kingdom and what it is in the earthly realm. However, people must receive a revelation of the Kingdom—God's Kingdom. Additionally, many people do not have an accurate representation of the Kingdom of God, which is why people are not experiencing the fullness of God. Many are not walking in the trueness of all of who God is and His desires for His children.

To clearly define the Kingdom of God, we must acknowledge God's only begotten Son, Jesus. He is the "King of kings and Lord of lords" (Rev. 19:16). He is the King of God's Kingdom, and He rules over it. Although God's Kingdom is spiritual and cannot be seen with natural lenses, it manifests itself in the physical. Most importantly, the Kingdom represents God.

The Bible also highlights those who are His adopted sons. Adopted sons of God are individuals who received Jesus Christ as their Lord and Savior. When one accepts Christ into their life, they are adopted into a relationship with the Father and His Kingdom. As an adopted child of God, you are a citizen of His Kingdom and commissioned to represent and manifest His Kingdom on the Earth.

Protocols of the Kingdom

Ephesians 2:19-22 is an essential scriptural reference of the Kingdom of God. The Scripture states, "Now, therefore, you are no longer strangers and foreigners, but fellow citizens with the saints and members of the household of God, having been built on the foundation of the apostles and prophets, Jesus Christ Himself being the chief *cornerstone,* in whom the whole building, being fitted together, grows into a holy temple in the Lord, in whom you also are being built together for a dwelling place of God in the Spirit." The said Scripture is a blueprint of what the protocol and standard of the Kingdom of God should be here on Earth. However, due to worldly influences and sin-like nature, such is not being replicated nor represented.

As a nation, we must keep Christ at the center of all that we do and all that we are; Jesus must be our Chief Cornerstone. Therefore, our ways should be in the likeness of Christ. Instead, the root structure of this world is in direct opposition to Jesus and the things of the Kingdom. For instance, what God calls evil, the world deems as good. What is right in God's eye is blasphemous to the world. Coincidently, the world's progressive will to reject God's way, inadvertently leads to the fulfillment of Isaiah 5:20.

Due to direct opposition, many people struggle with understanding the Kingdom of God, including "church people." Therefore, there is an outpouring of the spirit of carnality, agnosticism, atheism, and religiousness. And not to mention, many familial ties and traditions are carnal. These groupings and the likes are worldly. Therefore, many tactics and efforts to deploy the Kingdom of Heaven and dispel the wickedness are ineffective. To properly hone in on the Kingdom of Heaven and make room for Heaven to meet Earth, you must live by the protocols, standard, structure, and order of the Kingdom of Heaven. Carnality and lukewarmness will not suffice. You must be set apart in the Lord.

Standards of the Kingdom of Heaven

The Kingdom of God operates by a spiritual standard. So people who do not know the Kingdom do not know the standards of God. God has established a standard of holiness, righteousness, excellence, purity, unity, and order. When you are within the standards and the structure of the Kingdom, you will notice a spirit of unity. The spirit of unity is a standard that promotes civility, love, and harmony. The standard of unity advances the laws and the commands of God.

Although the world is chaotic, lost, and confused, there is still a system of order. The world has a system of government, laws, and policies. For example, in the workplace, there are specific codes of standards. Although, at times, codes and standards are violated, and inequality is prevalent, they were established for a reason. For example, speed limits and traffic lights are an example of a system of governance. Systems of law are designed to keep harmony, order, some kind of civility, and safety.

When you understand the law according to God, you recognize that it promotes unity, good, and personal well-being. However, when you are a wicked, rebellious, stiff-necked, stubborn, and an independent person, most likely, you will not be receptive to the laws. You will not understand nor respect the law, so you will reject it. As a result, people often get in trouble in the natural sense, with man, and spiritually with God.

Remember, just as there are consequences for breaking laws and statutes in the natural realm, there are consequences for disobeying God. The Bible gives us laws, commands, statutes, ordinances, and principles. When we believe in God's Word and apply it, it produces fruit in our life.

According to the Kingdom

When you know, work, and function according to the Kingdom, blessings will always be the result. You will always have progress; you will always have results that are for the glory of God. Also, when operating according to the Kingdom, your results will always be for your good (see Rom. 8:28). However, when you do not learn this truth, failure is in your destiny.

You must know that we are a royal priesthood, a holy nation (1 Pet. 2:9). As a whole, we are a great cloud of witnesses. And as ambassadors of the Kingdom of Heaven, we must function as a knit unit of the Lord. How can you be fully functioning and not connected to the body? Think about it, if my hand was cut from my arm, how can my hand function and survive if it is not connected to my body? Therefore, if God calls you a foot, be the foot God has created you to be. Every part of the body is significant.

Spiritual leadership is no more important than you. The only difference between spiritual leaders and general members of the Body, are their roles and responsibilities. Other than that, every joint supplies and every member causes growth for the body to edify itself in love (Eph. 4:16).

To further my point, Ephesians 4:11-14 says, "He Himself gave some *to be* apostles, some prophets, some evangelists, and some pastors and teachers, for the equipping of the saints for the work of ministry, for the edifying of the body of Christ, till we all come to the unity of the faith and of the knowledge of the Son of God, to a perfect man, to the measure of the stature of the fullness of Christ; that we should no longer be children, tossed to and fro and carried about with every wind of doctrine, by the trickery of men, in the cunning craftiness of deceitful plotting." You must know that God established His Kingdom to advance and uplift His children and His purposes. Therefore, He has positioned functioning ambassadors to carry and fulfill the missions He set before us.

Jesus, The Christ

When you are pushing the agenda of the Kingdom, it may prove to be challenging. Most people are either unbelieving or agnostic, have preconceived notions about life, or are stuck in religion and tradition. Therefore, difficulty seeing the Kingdom will arise. According to the Bible, you must be "born again" to enter the Kingdom. If you are not a born-again believer, you will not have a revelation of the Kingdom of Heaven. Thus, sharing the Gospel with unbelievers may prove to be challenging because they do not have a revelation of God nor His Kingdom.

You must be "born again" and "born of water and the Spirit" (John 3:3; 3:5). When a person is born again, the light switch of their spirit is turned on. God awakens the spirit man to receive knowledge of the spiritual world.

In John 3, Nicodemus went to Jesus at night. Nicodemus not only came in physical darkness but spiritual darkness. All who come to Jesus do so with spiritual blindness. When a person's spiritual light switch is turned on, they come to a place of spiritual recognition. The light of Christ provides a place of spiritual awareness where you become sensitive, have an awakening, and have an eye-opening revelation of the spiritual world, particularly the Spirit of God.

You cannot see the Kingdom of Heaven until The Holy Spirit awakens your spirit. The transaction of becoming born again must take place so that you can be saved. However, you must be born of water and of spirit to enter the Kingdom of Heaven. John 3:6 says, "That which is born of the flesh is flesh, and that which is born of the Spirit is spirit."

Within the duration of Jesus's life, He lived a lifestyle of *death to life*. When you think about Jesus Christ, He should be examined from the revelation as Jesus, *The* Christ, not Jesus Christ. The name of Jesus Christ is not a simple connection of names. No. The name of Jesus Christ is significant to why Jesus is Christ. We are talking about Jesus, the man of flesh who died, but we are also talking about Christ, the one who resurrected. The life of Christ was a life of *death-to-life*.

The life of a person who is in the Kingdom of God will live a life of death-to-life. Jesus is our prototype. Jesus was crucified and resurrected; thus, we must do the same. We are to die to our flesh —

dying to self so that we can rise in the Holy Spirit of God. When we resurrect in the Holy Spirit, we are rising to the newness of life and resurrecting in Christ. Therefore, in our walk with God, we must have a revelation that we live a life of death-to-life.

The Power of the Kingdom

The Kingdom of God is not in word but power. Paul said in 1 Corinthians 2:4, "And my speech and my preaching were not with persuasive words of human wisdom, but in demonstration of the Spirit and of power." It is all about the demonstration. It is not about just articulation. When you consider Jesus, you see two things at work within Him: revelation and demonstration. Revelation and demonstration, not articulation, per se. Yes, we must be able to communicate, but what are we communicating?

When Jesus spoke, He spoke uniquely, distinct from what everybody else was saying and how they said it. When Jesus spoke, there was no doubt He was speaking as an oracle of God. However, when Paul spoke, he came from revelation, not what he conjured up, not based on his experience, not based on tradition, not based on affiliation, not based on what everyone else was doing nor saying. Paul never followed the model or way of man. Instead, Paul chose to do it the way God showed him.

We must posture ourselves in leading the way God shows us. We must speak what God reveals. When you are authentic, you do not have to imitate others. Yet many people walk as carbon copies of others because they think they should mimic others to be accepted and received. Leaders who demonstrate God's glory are uncommon. The excellency of Jesus and His demonstration to exert His leadership authority baffled the religious folks. Jesus's standards are what drew the world to Him. Those seeking answers, looking for a change, and looking for solutions saw that opportunity in Jesus.

If you are going to be like everyone, you are not operating the way God created you. God births authentic leaders. Those called by God are secure, comfortable, and confident in their identity. They will even be comfortable in their skin, their way of communicating, and their way of operating.

The Bible says, "Therefore by their fruits, you will know them"(Matt. 7:20). Matthew 7:20 proves that leadership is not all about articulation but rather revelation and demonstration. See, you must have a genuine leader that is demonstrating the Kingdom of God, according to Jeremiah 3:15, "And I will give you shepherds according to My heart, who will feed you with knowledge and understanding." Your God-sent leader will have a heart like God and desires the best for everybody. Your leader will not speak to your comfort zones but will speak into your spirit. After all, God is more concerned about our spirit than anything else.

There is a story in the Word of God about the seven sons of Sceva (see Acts 19:11-20). They were trying to imitate what they saw Apostle Paul doing. However, they did not have revelation and the power of the Spirit. As a result, the evil spirit said, "Jesus I know, and Paul I know; but who are you?" The Bible says the man who had the evil spirit attacked them, which ended with wounds. Acts 19:11-20 is the epitome of why it is paramount to have revelation and demonstration.

A true spiritual leader demonstrates the Kingdom and servanthood and exemplifies the heart of God. More importantly, as we see in Acts 19:11-20, leaders demonstrate authority for the good of God's will. They do not utilize their power to manipulate. God-ordained leaders know their power and authority are for the works of dismantling the devil, setting the captives free, and empowering people to walk as God created them. If your leader is not helping you walk in freedom by overcoming strongholds, addictions, and the enemy's attacks, you are not submitted to leaders of excellence. If you are not connected to God-ordained leaders, free yourself. Free yourself and find leaders who carry the revelation and demonstrate the power and authority that can help you maintain your freedom and salvation.

God does not want you to be under leadership who will control you. Instead, God wants you submitted to leaders who will launch you. We must grasp the fact that we do not belong to our leaders. We belong to God. I have two grown kids, and my children do not belong to me;

they belong to God. A real leader will always make sure you understand that you belong to God.

Leaders must realize that they have a role and responsibility to you, but they do not own nor should they try to control you. Leaders must have a profound responsibility and accountability to God and be accountable and responsible to you. The mandatory traits of leaders are to walk you into freedom, bring you into wholeness, elevate and edify you, and build you into all God created and called you to be.

Leaders should never try to marginalize you nor attempt to put you under them. So if your leader is not helping to develop you into working what God put in you by edifying you, which may not always feel comfortable, then something is utterly wrong.

The Kingdom of Heaven Is Within You

Recently, I have heard a leader say, "I was in church, and I asked, why am I here? I do not want to be here. I hate being here." Those remarks were said because there was no substance in the church. They knew that being there was not going to change anything. If nothing is happening at home then, nothing is going to happen in the House of God. It will take some people who will be authentic and raw to lead people into the presence of God and victory in Christ.

The mentality of many people is, "You have to make me feel good and give me what I want. You have to give me food and clothes and tell me what I want to hear. Pastor, that is your job." People have reduced church and the things of God down to the notion of thinking they are owed something. The Word says we are seated in heavenly places with Christ Jesus (see Eph. 2:6). But the House of God, the church, religion, and everything else has been reduced to nothing. And the church has very little to no impact on the world.

According to the Word of God, we are to go into all the world and make disciples. It does not say "go into the four walls of the church;" it says "go to all the world." If I am not mistaken, the Bible references the *Kingdom* over 260 times and mentions *church* a couple of times. We should not be so focused on the church when God is focused on Kingdom. The church is an earthly extension or representation of the Kingdom and is not God's priority. The priority is getting people into His Kingdom.

When you are doing Kingdom business, you know about the revelation of the Holy Spirit. When you have the revelation of the Holy Spirit, it is not about you going to the church, because you know the church is everywhere you go. The Kingdom of Heaven is within you.

I hear God asking, do you know Me? And are you doing what I put you here to do? Are you fulfilling My assignment with the gifts I gave you? God is highly concerned about your affairs, your focus, and your priorities.

Revolve Around Christ

The structure of this world is like a pyramid. There are very few at the top of the pyramid, and the mass majority are at the bottom. Unfortunately, the worldly system is not the only system structured like a pyramid; religion and some churches have succumbed to this method of operation. When you look at some religious entities and churches, the amount of people holding a rank in leadership positions and authority decreases at the top. The pyramid structure is to keep the masses at the bottom to uphold those at the top. Ephesians 2:19-22 dispels this ungodly standard, called the world system that religion has replicated.

On the contrary, an analogy of the Kingdom of God can be the planet. Within this planet, there is a core. The core represents Jesus. Around the core is a foundation. View the foundation as offices, which belong to the officials of the Kingdom who are to represent Jesus Christ. The foundational offices are called the *five-fold ministry*. Ephesians 2:20 says, "Having been built on the foundation of the apostles and prophets, Jesus Christ Himself being the chief cornerstone." The foundation of the Kingdom of Heaven here on Earth begins with the apostles and prophets. Next, the evangelists, pastors, and teachers.

The world is supposed to revolve around the Kingdom. If the world is supposed to revolve around the Kingdom, then the world must revolve around Christ. God intended everything to revolve around Christ and those He delegated to administer His heart, will, and way for the world. God revealed His structure and protocol to demonstrate and impart His will to His servants and the world.

The Core is Jesus. Around the core is the five-fold ministry. Next, you have the whole world that is supposed to revolve around the Core and the five-fold. Granted, the world revolves around neither.

Likewise, our physical bodies are likened to the description of Earth. The core of every person is a spirit. Around the core is a soul. Our body is a representation of Christ here on Earth. And individually, we are all connected. It is a rippling effect. It begins with the spirit, which is supposed to influence the soul. As a result, the soul influences the body. Jesus Christ, the center of this world, is supposed to impact the world through His five-fold ministers. And around the five-fold ministry is the whole body.

Sadly, a vast number of people struggle with the truth that Jesus Christ is the center of this world and the only way to God. Additionally, many struggles with the idea that God handpicks and appoints rulers of this world to carry out His purpose and assignments. Many are rebellious and believe that control and liberty should rest in their hands and authority. For some, it is a tough pill to swallow. However, as nations are comprised of governmental systems, such is so within the realm of the Kingdom of Heaven.

When considering the leadership within a governmental system, there are leaders, yet their leadership positions are not supreme. The leaders within this earthly realm hold a certain level of leadership but do not retain all authority. Jesus said, "All authority has been given to Me in heaven and on Earth. Go therefore and make disciples" (Matt. 28:18-19). *Who is Jesus talking to?* Jesus is talking to all who believe in Him and especially those He placed into leadership. All authority has been delegated to His officials to use on His behalf as His representatives. Not only do they have His authority, but they also have His heart, mind, and perspective on how to carry out the Kingdom of God within the earth.

Just as we represent Jesus Christ here on Earth, we also partake in some sufferings as He did. Although Jesus said things that astounded people and performed wondrous acts, He still faced persecution. When you truly walk with God, you will have many people who mock you and misunderstand you. Never make the mistake of thinking that you will not face opposition from your peers and elders.

Even more so, be watchful for false praise and admonition. Acts 16:16-18 talks of a girl possessed with the spirit of divination, yet she proclaimed false praises to Paul and Silas. As a child of God and a leader, you must be mindful of who claps at your accomplishments and who praises you. Just as Paul and Silas encountered the demon-possessed girl who gave them false accolades and Jesus experienced a deceitful kiss from Judas, you must remain watchful of the same. You must not be ignorant of the various forms of persecution and opposition.

Notes

Connect with Carlton Evans

Business and Ministry Support Portal

Business & Ministry Support Portal (B&M SP) serves businesses, ministries, families, and individuals. We provide spirit-filled & bible-based ministry services and financial assistance. With this business, you can be both a giver or requester of ministry services or financial aid. To find out more about B&M SP visit our Facebook Page.

www.facebook.com/businessandministrysupportportal

For business and ministry inquiries, please contact Carlton at businessandministrysp@gmail.com or by phone at (703) 477-5130.

The Kingdom Leadership Academy

The Kingdom Leadership Academy is a Bible-based academic training center offering online instruction, mentoring, and experiential guidance in all areas of Kingdom Leadership.

Featuring, we offer online college-level bible school courses and mini-courses for individualized learning and award credentials. To learn more about The Kingdom Leadership Academy, visit:

www.carltoncevans.com

Books by Carlton Christ Evans, Jr.

Manhood, Husbandhood, Fatherhood

•

What is means to be Awakened, Empowered, and Enlighted by God

•

God Created Marriage

•

Kingdom Leadership
(Formerly Spiritual Leadership Manual)

Made in the USA
Middletown, DE
25 March 2023

26961189R00060